Distributors:

UNITED STATES: *Kodansha International/USA, Ltd., through Harper & Row, Publishers, Inc., 10 East 53rd Street, New York, 10022.* SOUTH AMERICA: *Harper & Row, Publishers, Inc., International Department.* CANADA: *Fitzhenry & Whiteside Limited, 150 Lesmill Road, Don Mills, Ontario.* MEXICO AND CENTRAL AMERICA: *HARLA S. A. de C. V., Apartado 30–546, Mexico 4, D. F.* UNITED KINGDOM: *Phaidon Press Limited, Littlegate House, St. Ebbe's Street, Oxford OX1 1SQ.* EUROPE: *Boxerbooks Inc., Limmatstrasse 111, 8031 Zurich.* AUSTRALIA AND NEW ZEALAND: *Book Wise (Australia) Pty. Ltd., 104–8 Sussex Street, Sydney 2000.* THE FAR EAST: *Toppan Company (S) Pte. Ltd., Box 22 Jurong Town Post Office, Jurong, Singapore 22.*

Published by Kodansha International Ltd., 2–12–21 Otowa, Bunkyo-ku, Tokyo 112 and Kodansha International/USA, Ltd., 10 East 53rd Street, New York, New York 10022 and 44 Montgomery Street, San Francisco, California 94104. Copyright © 1968 by Kodansha International Ltd. All rights reserved. Printed in Japan.

LCC 68–17456
ISBN 0–87011–052–7
JBC 0325-780518-2361

First edition, 1968
Ninth printing, 1978

CONTENTS

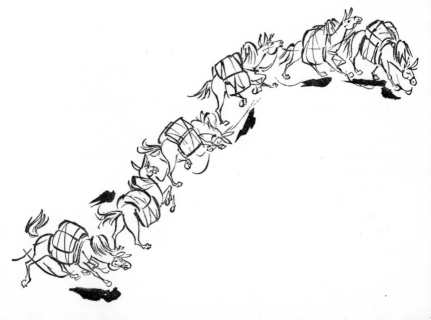

NOTE ON THE ENGLISH TEXT

In rendering Mr. Kazami's text into English, I have used the spellings for Nepalese names that seemed most familiar to English-speaking readers. It must be borne in mind, however, that the various Nepalese languages have a number of sounds that cannot be transliterated into English (or any tongue using the Latin language) with great exactness. Spellings, therefore, are sometimes hardly more than approximations of sounds. In general, vowels are pronounced as they are in Italian, and "h" does not combine with other consonants (save in "sh" and "ch," which have much the same sound as in English) but receives its own, fairly strong aspiration.

I should like to express my deep indebtedness to the Royal Nepalese Embassy in Tokyo, which very kindly supplied much of the background material for Mr. Kazami's account of his journey.

— J. G.

THE HIMALAYAS
A JOURNEY TO NEPAL

In 1958 I spent a couple of months in Nepal, where I fell in love—
with Nepal.

In the postscript to my book, "Nepalese Mountains and People," published in 1960, I wrote:

"You don't have to climb a mountain in Nepal to experience
the beauty of the country. There is something indescribably
delightful in just wandering around the countryside with a
small party, the great mountains towering above you. You can
camp wherever you like, and since there is food to eat everywhere you don't need a lot of porters.

"I think if I were to stay for a short time in one of the many
beautiful farms that dot the lower slopes of the Himalayas, I
could make a most exciting and interesting documentary film.
Some day, perhaps, I will have the opportunity to go back to
Nepal and live for a time with her giants. How I long for that
chance! It is like a glorious and persistent dream—will it ever
come true?"

Good fortune did not desert me: six years later, my dream became
reality.

Since it was, in all truth, the chance of my lifetime, I determined to stay as long as possible, wandering about alone, with only porters and guides, taking as many pictures as I could—for to me it is even more exciting to photograph a mountain than to climb it, although most of the time, of course, I couldn't do the one without having first done the other.

I arrived in Nepal, for the second time, in September, 1964, and stayed there till May of the following year, and it was during these nine months that I took most of the photographs in this book.

My favorite camera for mountain work is a 4×5 Crown Graphic, but I also used a Zeiss Ikon (6×9), a Mamiya C-3 with a telephoto lens of 180 mm., and a Rolleiflex Automat F2.8. I brought with me also auxiliary lenses, filters, flash bulbs, and tripods, in addition to some two thousand rolls of film, both color and black-and-white, which were packed in two tea-boxes along with a Japanese desiccant called Shirikageru, to protect the film from dampness.

I had the black-and-white film developed, eventually, in Kathmandu; there would be no time, as I well knew, for me to develop it myself while on the march. The color film I had to have developed in Tokyo. I feared there might be deterioration because of the length of time that elapsed after exposure—but my fears, as it turned out, were groundless.

One of my porters carried a 4×5 camera attached to a tripod and always ready. As some of the country I crossed (particularly around Muktinath, north of Annapurna) was very dry at the time I was there, cameras and filters often got covered with dust. The camera could be cleaned with a brush, of course, but the filter had

THE HIMALAYAS 𝇊

into four states among his four heirs, and these dynasties held power until the Gurkha conquest in 1768. They vied amongst themselves in building many of the country's most beautiful temples and palaces and in enticing to their courts the best musicians and poets.

But it was this very rivalry that prevented their achieving a concerted plan of action to meet Prithwi Narayan, King of the Gurkhas, who in 1766 set out on his campaign of conquest that put an end to this golden age of Nepal. Under his less fiery successors, the country gradually deteriorated until, in 1816, it bowed—after a bloody struggle—to the superior might of the British under General Ochterlony. By the terms of the treaty of Sagauli, Nepal ceded parts of the Terai and agreed to a British residency in Kathmandu.

In the 1840's Jung Bahadur rose to power, an extraordinary young man who killed all his enemies in what was known as the Kot massacre, and who remained in power until his death in 1878. He was the first major Hindu ruler to visit the West—in 1850, he called on Queen Victoria in London. As Prime Minister, he became, in actual fact, dictator of the country, and when in 1856 he made himself a maharaja, he established a hereditary line of prime ministers who were dictators also, for the kings of Nepal were forced to accede to their superior power and became mere titular monarchs.

One of this line, Chandra Shumsher, who ruled as Prime Minister between 1901 and 1929, was like the others a despot, but he was also an enlightened, forward-thinking man who reformed the government service, built roads, and installed electricity and telephones. His successors, however, were not of his calibre, and once to be changed. When atmospheric conditions were wrong, I was sometimes unable to take pictures at dawn or sunset, and often, naturally, I had to wait for just the right second. Yet, despite the hardships of mountain travel and the occasional frustrations, the whole experience was the most delightful and fascinating of my life—and I am still in love.

Nepal, in at least one way, is like Japan: until 1950 she wrapped herself behind a screen of national isolation that was similar to Japan's during the Tokugawa period.

Very little is known about the earliest history of Nepal, although there is probably a wealth of material preserved in the old temples and shrines that has not yet even begun to be scientifically investigated. The general assumption is that from around the seventh to the first century B.C., the country was ruled by the Kirantis (ancestors of present-day Nepalese tribes), and that it was one of these rulers who introduced Buddhism into Nepal. Those who succeeded the Kirantis came for the most part, it seems, from India and continued to adhere to Buddhism; but the whole story of these centuries remains dark and shadowy, and it is not until the beginning of the thirteenth century, when Abhaya-Malla instituted an orthodox Hindu dynasty, that details become sharper.

After a turbulent period of wars and invasions, the seventh raja of the Rajput dynasty, Jayastithi-Malla, achieved a degree of peace: he established a legal code for the country and partitioned the entire population, Buddhists included, into a strict caste system, according to profession. The eighth raja, Yaksha-Malla, divided the kingdom

9

2. *Pokhara*, a green and fertile village on a plateau twenty-five hundred feet above sea level, offers a fantastic panorama of the Annapurna range, whose peaks rise sheerly to heights of over twenty-six thousand feet. (*see previous page, inside foldout*)

◄3. *New Year's Day* is a major festival in the Himalayas. Here, at the Monastery of Thangboche, a masked lama brandishes a sword, to drive away evil spirits, as he dances to the local music. The bright, cheerful sounds banish for a time the deep silence that reigns over the highest mountains in the world.

again the government of the country degenerated into sloth and corruption. All revenues from taxes, for example, went directly into the pockets of the prime ministers and their families who built great palaces for themselves while the rest of the country suffered.

Clearly this was not a situation that could long endure—and, after the Second World War, after India's independence, after China's march into Tibet, Nepal found that she too was faced with revolutionary change. In 1951, the last prime minister of the line abdicated, and King Tribhuvan returned from his Indian exile. When he died in 1956, Crown Prince Mahendra Bir Bikram Shah Deva (a direct descendant of Prithwi Narayan, who conquered the country in 1768) rose to the throne.

Nepal became a member of the United Nations, opened diplomatic relations with a number of hitherto unrecognized countries, and prepared to hold the first election in her long history. This, in a nation where ninety-five per cent of the population was illiterate, and where the terrain is so varied, and so much of it is inaccessible, was no mean feat—yet it was carried off.

The elections of May, 1959, offered new hope for democracy—but these hopes were soon shattered by the party elected, which began a systematic return to the despotism of earlier eras. National feeling ran so strongly that on December 15, 1960, King Mahendra dismissed the Council of Ministers and dissolved the parliament. The next twenty-eight months were spent in evolving a new system of democracy that would blend with the national sentiment and provide the country with the mechanics of government capable of leading it toward modernization.

This system of democracy was called *panchayat* and was designed

to secure the participation of the people in all levels of government. Based on the historical traditions of the country, *panchayat* is unlike a parliamentary form of government. It is a four-tier organization, the basic unit being the village *panchayat,* of which there are over 3,500, 14 city *panchayats,* 75 district *panchayats,* and 14 zonal *panchayats.* Responsible to this broad representative spectrum is the National Panchayat, in which the authority of all the other *panchayats* is invested. Another remarkable feature of the system was the formation of various class organizations and the election of representatives from these organizations to represent them at the National Panchayat.

And in the early 1960's, the gates of Nepal were again thrown open to all those alpinists whose only real aim in life was to explore the vast white stretches of the High Himalayas.

❀   ❀   ❀

Since 1950, mountain climbers of many nations have competed for distinction in "conquering" these near inaccessible peaks. In that year, the first summit to be successfully assaulted was that of Annapurna, and a second major successful ascent was made in 1953, when the Hunt Expedition reached the top of Everest.

Other successful expeditions that might be mentioned are those of the British Alpine Club on Kanchenjunga (28,146 feet), of a Kenya group on Himalchuli (25,801 feet), of the Himalayan Committee of Geneva on Langtang Himal (23,750 feet) and Ganesh Himal (23,299 feet), and of the Ladies Scottish Club on Jugal Himal (23,240 feet)—all in 1955. In 1956, there were two more successful assaults, on Lhotse and Manaslu, and then followed several blank years until a British team reached the summit of Annapurna II in 1960.

Before then there had been many successful expeditions, of which a number were Japanese, but first, mention must be made of the Japanese Alpine Club expedition that finally, after several tries, reached the summit of Manaslu (26,658 feet) in 1956, and of the Keiō University Alpine Club that climbed Himalchuli in 1960.

So Nepal and her great giants are not complete strangers to us. Perhaps they have exerted such a tremendously strong fascination because Japan's mountains are really tiny tots by comparison.

A chain of mountains is formed, in the first place, at the line of junction where continents collide; this continental drift was first identified by Alfred Wegener, who noted that its occurrence in the history of the earth is cyclical. (When continents drift apart, the space between them deepens to a sea.)

Once, long ago, in the far, far distant past, the Indian subcontinent was separated from the Asian mainland by the so-called Himalayan Sea. Then, still in the very dim past, these two land blocks began to move toward each other: their last approach started some seventy million years ago, in the Mesozoic era, and resulted in the first of the Himalayas—the Tibetan marginal mountains as they have been called. Further collisions followed, over aeons of time and during the last, which occurred quite recently, under the eye of early man, the very highest peaks in the Himalayas were piled up: the only mountains on earth that rise to a height of over twenty-six thousand feet.

They are almost incredibly steep. The transverse gorges of the great rivers that cross them are among the deepest cuttings in the world. The summit of Annapurna, for instance, which is

THE HIMALAYAS 🌿

26,504 feet, is less than twenty-five miles, as the crow flies, from that of Dhaulagiri (26,811 feet), yet the river between them, the Kali Gandaki, is not even four thousand feet above sea level. Much the same is true of the Marsyandi, which flows between Annapurna and Manaslu.

The Himalaya chain extends for about 1,250 miles, from Kashmir in the west to Burma in the east, and separates the tropical Indian subcontinent from the central Asiatic plateau. There are few breaches in this nearly impenetrable mountain barrier.

During the eight months of winter, the winds blowing over the mountains from the north are dry, and humidity is low. It is then that dust will cake your lenses (as well as choke your throat), and you must cope with both—if you can. In the summer, moist southerly winds prevail, and after the moisture condenses, the great clouds burst to emit the downpours that characterize the monsoon season.

Himalayan glaciers are far less gigantic than might be expected, partly because of the low precipitation and partly because of the lack of fields of granular snow, called névé, which act as accumulators. The monsoons, which occur regularly in Nepal between June and September, apparently have little or no effect in the highest altitudes: that is why the very summit of Everest is black, with only scanty patches of snow.

Then, on the slopes of the high mountains, come the great snow masses which extend many thousands of feet. Below the snow line lie alpine pastures, then thick forests, and then, sometimes as high as ten thousand feet, the first human settlements—and the beginning, so to speak, of the Kingdom of Nepal.

The country is shaped rather like a long and narrow rectangle. It rises from the thickly populated, malarial Terai in the south, at the northern edge of the Ganges plain, through jungles and marshes inhabited by tigers and leopards, elephants and rhinoceroses, on toward the Siwalik hills, the southernmost of the Himalayan mountains. Some of these rise out of the plain, in sheer elevation, to a height of six thousand feet or more. They are covered with rain forests, and the country here is wild and deserted.

Just to the north lies the Mahabharat chain, with peaks as high as ten thousand feet: it is these that formed a southern defensive barrier for the Nepalese Midlands, offering protection against warlike incursions from the south and permitting the development of a characteristic culture and civilization. The Mahabharat country is very steep and not well populated, although, because of its low passes and transverse rivers, it is intersected by a number of important trade routes.

Beyond lie the Midlands, the heart and, in a sense, the soul of the country—protected in the south by the Mahabharat range and in the north by the High Himalayas. This midland area is extremely narrow, averaging only about fifty miles in width, and it is just over five hundred miles long. Its elevation, which varies from two to six thousand feet, affords a pleasant climate favorable to the growing of a varied crop, although its inhabitants have so far failed to fully exploit its potential. The mean January temperature of Kathmandu is 50° Fahrenheit, and the mean July temperature is 77°. Here in the Midlands live the most ancient of the Nepalese people and by far the largest percentage of the entire population: over three-quarters.

Then, with breathtaking steepness, out of the central plateau, rise the great giants—a seemingly impenetrable fortress against the world to the north. The only means of access between the Midlands and the Inner Himalayas that lie beyond the giants are the valleys around the unbelievably deep gorges of the great Himalayan rivers.

The Inner Himalayas, north of the principal chain, are high valleys shadowed on all sides by the far higher giants of the High Himalayas and of the Tibetan zone to the north.

Nepal lies between Longitude 80° and 88° East and Latitude 27° and 30° North. Thus, its climate, were it not for the high mountains, would be rather like Egypt's—but the high mountains are there, not to be ignored for a moment, and they contribute to the extreme diversity not only of the climate but also of the people. Nepal, with an area of only fifty-five thousand square miles and a population of less than ten million, is made up of a very large number of ethnic groups and minorities.

The original inhabitants appear to have been a negroid people, who were largely absorbed by immigrants from both north and east: the Dravidians, who are supposed to have been originally white, and yellow-skinned peoples from Indochina and Cambodia. Much later, only about three or four thousand years ago, they were joined by Aryans speaking an Indo-Germanic language. In the mountainous areas of Nepal, these various peoples encountered Mongoloid tribes from the interior of Asia, with whom they tended to mix, although in some more inaccessible areas certain of the groups have remained fairly pure.

At present, the Nepalese may be divided into two main categories: the Tibeto-Nepalese and the Indo-Nepalese, and the languages they speak, as well as the shape of their eyes, reflect their origins. Within the two large divisions, there may be distinguished a number of subdivisions of race and tribe scattered over the country. In general, it may be said that each ethnic group chose a familiar altitude to live in. The most ancient Nepalese groups are to be found in the Midlands, at the higher altitudes, and on the southern slopes of the Himalayas; the Indo-Nepalese occupy a large part of the Midlands as well as the whole of the Terai; the more purely Tibetan groups live far to the north, chiefly in the valleys of the Inner Himalayas.

Of the ancient Nepalese groups, the Newars are among the most interesting—for they are the architects of the Kingdom and built many of its great temples in the characteristic Nepalese pagoda style. They are excellent craftsmen—in stone, wood, and metal—and painters; their literature and mythology are extremely rich and varied, and they long ago developed their own system of writing. They are skilled, successful traders, and they are also good agriculturalists, although they make almost no use of the plough, preferring a short-handled iron hoe that has not changed its shape for thousands of years.

The Thamangs, another ancient Nepalese group, are descended, according to their mythology, from a cow that bore three sons, the youngest of whom became the father of the Thamang race. Their ancient religion was a kind of shamanism—they believed that the world around them was full of spirits with whom they might make contact by means of magical incantations. The magi cian Bon played a major role in this ancient belief, which is still adhered to in some of the more remote Thamang settlements. The Thamangs inhabit a wide range of altitudes; in some of the valleys of Ganesh Himal, they grow rice on the floor of the valley, grain at middle altitudes, and potatoes all the way up to the timber line.

THE HIMALAYAS ❧

The home of the Gurungs is the southern slope of the Annapurna massif, where they pasture their cattle (mainly water buf-
faloes) as high as twelve thousand feet. Most are Hindus, although
they still, in isolated settlements, worship the old local gods and
practice tantrism and even more ancient magic. Many Gurungs
have served with the British army in far-away places, and now,
back in Nepal, live a pleasant, indolent life on their pensions.

The Mangars, ethnologically related to the Newars, have, like
the Gurungs, achieved a reputation for bravery in the British army.
They are also well known as bridge-builders, miners, and black-
smiths. Although mainly Buddhists, they practice as well a kind
of tantric Hinduism. Their home is in western Nepal, but every
year they migrate south to the Terai, where they manufacture
bamboo baskets and mats to sell in the frontier markets, and then
north, to engage in the salt trade.

The Rais and the Limbus, usually thought of together as the
Kirantis, were the first people to live in the Nepal valley, according
to their own tradition. Rai men are known for their bravery; Rai
women, for their beauty. The Rais have developed a unique form
of courtship that still persists: a girl's suitor must, in the presence
of her parents, sing a song he has composed, and then the girl
must invent a response; if she cannot (as must, obviously, happen
sometimes by intention), then the boy has won his suit; if she
makes a response to which he cannot reply, he must consider that
he has been rejected. In Limbu mythology, God created first earth,
then water, and at last man—out of pure gold. But an envious,
horse-faced beast destroyed the first man. So God, as punishment,
made the horse walk on four legs and carry burdens; then He
created the second man—but this time out of ashes and dung.

The Indo-Nepalese were originally priests and monks who fled from the disturbed plains of Northern India, along with a number of warriors. With the help of these warriors, Brahmans from the south were able to impose their higher social rank, as well as a caste system, on the local Nepalese. Where they intermarried, their children were known as Khas, and it was the language these Khas developed that later came to be the official language of Nepal, known as Nepali, or "Gurkhali."

The other major ethnic group in Nepal is of Tibetan origin: Sherpas and Thakals belong to this group. They occupied the deserted regions in the higher altitudes of the Himalayas, such as the Inner Himalaya valleys, and settled along the main trade routes between India and Tibet. They speak their own language, which is akin to Tibetan, and practice a Tibetan lamaist form of Buddhism. I shall have more to say about these groups a little later, as they are the people with whom I had closest contact in my travels through the High Himalayas.

Obviously, many languages are spoken throughout the country, but Nepali is understood everywhere. English is the second language of the educated (who are few in number) and of those who fought with the British.

And obviously also, many religions are practiced, although mainly they are one form or another of either Hinduism or Buddhism. Nepal is a Hindu kingdom, yet it is also the birthplace of Lord Buddha, and Nepal's Hindus have accepted the Buddha as the ninth incarnation of their god Vishnu. Probably, as it works out, most Nepalese are willing to revere any of their country's religions, and to tolerate all of them. No one has ever heard two Nepalese quarrel because their names for God were not the same.

The people of Nepal are as friendly, honest, self-reliant, and hospitable a folk as may be found anywhere in the world—and perhaps one of the reasons for this rather remarkable catalogue of virtues is that the Nepalese have never undergone the painful experience of being colonized, either by Asians or Europeans. Another reason may lie in the fact that Nepal, like my own country, Japan, has some large and powerful neighbors who are not always friendly, so she has had to learn, like my own country, to protect her neutrality and her freedom and to cultivate her self-reliance.

Although crime and violence, we are told, are increasing almost everywhere in the world, they are still virtually unknown in Nepal. The poorest Sherpa, for instance, may be entrusted unhesitatingly with relatively large sums of money that major expeditions have to carry, to pay guides and porters. Although these expeditions, as well as smaller, more vulnerable parties (such as mine), must pass through enormous stretches of deserted mountain country, thefts or robberies have almost never been heard of.

And the Nepalese, like (I think I may say) the people of my own country, have that unfailing Asiatic gift of courtesy that can make life so very agreeable—if, at times, a bit unrealistic. The Nepalese are, in fact, so reluctant to impart news the hearer may find unpleasant, that sometimes it is very difficult to get any news at all! But surely the basic concept on which this national tendency depends is a desirable one: it indicates not only a profound self-respect but a profound respect also for all other men. It is perhaps the only basis for lasting peace in the world. And I think the world might do worse than let those kindly, intelligent, incredibly brave and honest mountain people of Nepal take charge of it!

My first glimpse of Nepal was from a plane winging its way out of India. Dhaulagiri, Annapurna, Manaslu, Everest unfolded their splendors before me, gleaming like a gigantic silver fortress in the sun, which I tried—alas! unsuccessfully—to photograph from the plane. It was hard for me to realize, as I looked at these great white giants through the window, quite how inaccessible they were. I was soon, however, to learn.

Communication within Nepal is still very primitive: most of the traveling you do, you do afoot. The capital, Kathmandu, where we alighted, is the largest city in the country, yet its population is hardly more than 120,000. In the whole green basin where Kathmandu lies, live only half a million people. There is a highway south to India and one north to Tibet (although the Tibetan frontier is closed) and, apart from these, only a few, not yet completed highways to east and west. Kathmandu boasts but eight hotels that the government recommends to tourists.

Once, just outside the city, I asked a man where he was going. "Nepal," he replied. It was only later I learned that the capital, with its green and wooded basin, is familiarly known all over the country as Nepal—for Kathmandu, which was founded in the year 723, was, for all practical purposes, until the beginning of the nineteenth century, Nepal itself. Its history was Nepal's history, and the Nepalese culture and civilization rose and flourished in the Kathmandu valley.

THE HIMALAYAS 🌿

"The major portion of Nepal," said Mr. Koirala, the Prime Minister, in 1960, "owing to a lack of efficient and comfortable means of transport and communication, is not yet open to the average tourist." Even today, tourists who want to visit parts of the country other than the capital must secure special permission from the Ministry of Foreign Affairs, which, in the labyrinthine, thousand-roomed Singha Durbar in Kathmandu, is not always easy to find!

Durbar Square, by the way, is a most exciting place to visit of a morning, when men and women, in their colorful and varied Nepalese dress, throng across it on their way to one or another of the many temples that border the square, each carrying a metal bowl with rice, vermilion, and flowers to offer to the gods.

Another exciting experience is an early morning bazaar in Kathmandu, where people come to sell and buy vegetables and fruits, milk and cheese, chickens and eggs, ready-cooked foods, staples like potatoes, rice, and grain, as well as firewood, and second-hand goods of every kind that look more like junk than anything worth buying or selling. Bartering is prolonged and voluble, and goes uninterruptedly on while an odd cow or two amble past, nibbling at a bit of green that is being offered for sale. The seller never grows angry at the cow or makes the slightest attempt to restrain her (though the green may be his livelihood for the day)— for the cow is as sacred to Nepal as she is to India.

Nor did anyone seem to object to the fact that I kept taking pictures all the time—though one night, when I wanted to photograph a temple, I heard a voice cry out of the darkness when my flash bulb went off. I scurried away, remembering the story of a fellow-photographer who was taking night pictures in a park.

After the flash, he heard a terrified female shriek: "Oh, let's go! It's lightning!"

The back streets of Kathmandu are a fascinating jumble of old houses, with elegantly carved figures on their wooden posts and windowsills. I used to love to wander through these lanes, glutting my eyes on the beauty of line and color. Once, when I was talking to Yamagawa, the artist, we both agreed that the back streets of Kathmandu were more exciting than those of Paris. Then we had to confess to each other that neither of us had ever been to Paris—and dissolved into laughter at the nonsense that we'd been talking. . . .

Kathmandu was known as Kantipur until the beginning of the sixteenth century, when, according to legend, the tree of Paradise (the Kalpa-briksha) came to the city and, in human guise, mingled with the people who were watching a procession. One of the spectators recognized the man-shaped tree, took hold of him, and would not let him go until he promised to provide another tree big enough to build a whole house out of. Four days later, this perspicacious spectator was granted the gift he had demanded, an enormous sal-tree, out of which he built himself a dwelling that still stands in the center of the city. It was then that Kathmandu received its present name, for *kath* means "wood" and *mando*, "house."

Aside from this miraculous dwelling, there are many temples in the city, both Buddhist and Hindu of course, as there are also in the neighboring towns of Bhaktapur and Patan: in all, some

23

two thousand in the whole area. It is almost impossible to make a precise distinction between Nepalese Buddhists and Hindus, or to tell whose temple is whose. Some groups, to be sure, like the Bhotiyas, are purely Buddhist, and some Brahman groups are orthodox Hindus, but most of the people worship both the Buddha and the Hindu gods as well as a great variety of very ancient deities and spirits—and the grand magicians of tantrism too! To the Nepalese, attempts to make distinctions among the various gods they worship seem absurd. (In this respect, too, they are perhaps a bit like us Japanese.) In the Swayambhu Nath Sanctuary, near Kathmandu, images of the Buddha, of Jesus, and of Mahatma Gandhi stand beside those of the Hindu gods.

The Indian emperor, Ashoka, is said to have come to Patan to propagate Buddhism and to have erected there four of those famous *stupas* of his that mark sites holy to Buddhists, yet in the very center of the town stands a Hindu temple sacred to Krishna. Nepalese Buddhism, like the Tibetan, is of the Mahayana sect: it has lamas and monasteries and prayer-wheels with the familiar formula, *om mani padme hum* (which has been rendered into English as "Hail to the jewel in the lotus").

Architecturally too, the temples are extremely difficult to distinguish, for most of them are built in the pagoda style. This is said to be an exclusively Nepalese contribution to architecture—it was a Newar, so the story goes, who built the famous white pagoda in far-away Peking.

Of all the many Hindu temples in Kathmandu, the holiest perhaps is Pashupati Nath, which is said also to be the oldest building in Asia. It stands on the right bank of the Bagmati, a holy river, and is guarded by a massive bronze bull. On the left bank of the same river stands the temple of Guheswari, which contains no image of a god or goddess but merely an aperture where worshipers may pour water, or stronger drink, offer eggs, and sprinkle vermilion and rice. The Buddhist shrine of Swayambhu Nath lies high on a hill, with an approach of four hundred steps, and houses what may well be the world's largest gilded image of the Buddha. It is said to be some two thousand years old. In yet another temple of Kathmandu, a baby girl (chosen with great care by the priests) is worshiped as the goddess Kumari until she reaches the age of puberty. (I don't know what happens to her then!) To name but one more, out of the many shrines in the city, there is that which houses the image of Machhindra: it is drawn in solemn procession through the streets of Kathmandu every March and symbolizes peace—to both Hindus and Buddhists.

Nor do the neighboring towns of Patan and Bhaktapur lack their share of artistic treasures. Patan, by the way, is often called Lalitpur, and Bhaktapur has frequently gone under the name of Bhatgaon, but both cities, under whatever name, are lovely to wander through.

Patan is, in a sense, the artistic capital of Nepal; its artists have been famous through the centuries, not only for their architecture, but also for their wood carving, metal work, and stone inlay. The city was founded, according to tradition, by the famous Buddhist emperor Ashoka, who is also said to have built the *stupas* that stand at the four corners of the city. In strict fact, however, these are probably not burial mounds at all, but *chaitiyas* that symbolize the four ages of the world. The most remarkable building in Patan is the stone temple of Krishna, built in 1630, with a great colonnade and a fascinating, intricate series of carvings of scenes from the Ramayana and Mahabharat epics.

The chief sight of Bhaktapur is the famous gateway to the temple of Taleju, built by the last of the Malla rulers; it has been called "the most lovely piece of art in the whole kingdom." *Bhakta* means "devotee"—hence the name, Bhaktapur, city of devotees—and there are numerous, beautifully carved shrines and temples, as well as the lavish and impressive Durbar Square, with its many Malla monuments.

But I had not come to Nepal to see only the man-made glory of her buildings—I had come to pay homage to her giants, and now that the monsoon season was ended, I could start on my pilgrimage.

I had heard horrendous tales of the monsoons—of rivers in spate, demolished bridges, and stranded travelers at the mercy of the elements and a peculiarly loathsome gift of nature called the leech. He is a small beast with, apparently, a genuine fondness for human beings and who contrives to wriggle through the tiniest openings in clothing or shoes. Once he has got his suckers into you, he drinks your blood, and only after he has had what he thinks is enough, is he willing to fall off. If you pull him out, his suckers remain inside you, and the wound grows infected and painful. Even if you let him drink his fill, the wound he has made will go on bleeding for hours, for he secretes a fluid that prevents coagulation. No one who has not experienced him can imagine quite how disagreeable he is.

But the monsoons, while they make communication impossible within the country, also supply her with one of her staple foods, for it is during the heavy rains that the rice-growers do most of their work, singing all the while. The fields of the country grow green, and the myriad wild flowers burst suddenly into bloom.

But now, the monsoon season ended, I left Kathmandu early one beautiful autumn morning for Pokhara, accompanied by a Sherpa named Pemba.

The Sherpas are indispensable companions for any high mountain climbing in this part of the world. So essential are they, in fact, that each Sherpa who works as a mountain guide has what is called a "service book," where his qualifications and accomplishments are written down in detail for any prospective employers. The government "Sherpa Association" in Kathmandu is also at their disposal.

Along with the Thakals, the Sherpas apparently came originally from eastern Tibet (*shar* means "east," and *pa*, "people"). They settled in the valleys and the trading routes between India and Tibet, and there they prospered.

Sherpa villages are spread-out affairs, with ample, two-storied farmhouses under gabled roofs. Their animals are housed and their tools stored on the ground floor, while the upper story is one large room with the hearth in a corner. It is here that every visitor is conducted, for Sherpa hospitality is generous, and the wooden jug of *chang* (a home-brewed rice beer) is passed around; and it is here, by the hearth, that the family lives its life, eating and drinking, laughing and singing and telling tales, the men doing their business, the women nursing their young. Staple foods are rice, *tsampa* (barley meal eaten dry or stirred into milk), and potatoes. The Sherpas make a flavorsome dish called *gurr* out of grated raw potatoes mixed with butter and seasonings and baked on a heated stone.

THE HIMALAYAS ❧

Yaks are a symbol of Sherpa wealth and position, and many mountain guides invest their savings in herds of these cattle, from which they obtain their milk and their butter as well as their wool. The most highly prized animals are cross-breeds—high mountain and Nepalese cattle—for only the *zhum*, the female offspring of cross-breeding is fertile. Although forbidden by their religion to slaughter animals, the Sherpas are very fond of smoked yak meat, and so they import butchers from Tibet for the slaughtering.

Like many Nepalese Buddhists, the Sherpas practice a Tibetan form of lamaism, and their monasteries are, as formerly in Tibet, the chief centers of their learning. Many prosperous Sherpas have private temples in their own houses. They are a deeply religious people and are often at prayer. They believe in the doctrine of reincarnation, when the good and the evil done in a previous life are tallied and the prospects for a new life fixed. Eventually, the Sherpas believe, if a man succeeds in leading enough good lives, he may be freed of the necessity for further reincarnation—though he may decide to return to earth again and serve his fellow-men as a lama. The abbot of Tengpoche, the most famous of Sherpa monasteries, is believed to be a voluntary reincarnation. This deep practical belief in the rewards that accrue from having led a good life no doubt accounts, at least in part, for the absence of crime among the Sherpas; they preach respect for, and charity toward, all men—and they practice what they preach.

Yet they are by no means puritanical. Their sexual life is astonishingly free. No adult unmarried Sherpa, of either sex, is expected to be continent; no sense of shame or guilt attaches to casual relationships; and illegitimate children suffer no disadvantages. Young Sherpas, both boys and girls, are fully expected to "play the field" before they settle down to marriage. Nor is infidelity grounds for divorce, although the wronged man may exact a payment of thirty rupees (about four dollars) from his wife's seducer. If he chooses to ignore the incident (as he usually does), then they all sit down and drink some *chang* together and forget the whole thing. Either partner to a marriage may request a divorce; if the husband opposes it, then his successor must pay a compensation of about five dollars. Sometimes a Sherpa woman will have several husbands, or sometimes she will marry two brothers—a practice that ensures the presence of at least one man in the house despite the necessarily prolonged absences of mountain traders. If a woman does take several husbands, one is never jealous of the other, and the children are the children of all.

Pemba, the Sherpa who was going with me to Pokhara, was rather simple and easy-going—too much so, I feared, to take charge of the porters that I would eventually need. He kept looking, I noticed, at a photograph, and I finally asked him what he was studying so intently. He handed me the photograph—it was a picture of a woman. "Is she your mother?" I asked. No, she was his fiancee, he said, and he had often slept with her. "Are you going to marry her?" I asked. He smiled. "I no know," he answered.

Pokhara lies on a plateau some twenty-five hundred feet above sea level, under the shadow of the awesome Annapurna range and of sharp-crested Machha Puchhare—the fish-tailed mountain. Unfortunately, the afternoon we arrived, the clouds hung heavily over them, and there was little to be seen—and nothing to be photographed.

There are two Tibetan-style hotels in Pokhara, The Annapurna and The Sun and Snow, near the grassland airport. I got permission from The Sun and Snow to pitch my tent in their garden.

Very soon porters came looking for work. But they wanted sixteen rupees (over two dollars) a day, which was too much. The last time I was there, I told them, I paid only five rupees. So our bargaining started, and it went on all afternoon and evening, by which time there were ten prospective porters hanging about The Sun and Snow Hotel garden and they had lowered their price to fourteen rupees. At the end of the second day, they came down to ten. Finally, on the third day, we all agreed to eight. They claimed this was the lowest wage they had ever accepted that time of year—but they said it was better than nothing at all.

Some alpinists, I was told, had already started up the mountains from Pokhara. I knew also that Kyoto University's Alpine Club hoped to conquer Ganesh Himal that year.

The morning after our arrival, the sun rose clear in the sky, and the great mountains reared their crests in the bright morning glow. It was an unforgettable sight, which I tried to capture on film. On the plain of Pokhara is sub-tropical vegetation, with orange and banana trees; then, only fifty miles away, with no interlying range, rise the fantastically sheer, snowy peaks of the Annapurna range, with Dhaulagiri on the left, and on the right, to the east, Manaslu, Ganesh Himal, and Langtang Himal. On a clear day, standing in the plain of Pokhara, you can see the massive giants of the Himalayas to a distance of over a hundred and fifty miles!

That same day, I took some pictures of Pokhara, a charming little town, with trees and flowers everywhere, and the Seti river gushing through a deep canyon not far away. The town is a trading center, where people come from all the nearby regions as well as from far-away Tibet and India, to buy and sell. Bargaining is animated—and sometimes violent, for Indian traders have a reputation for dishonesty.

The people are mainly Newars, a slender and graceful race, with almond-shaped eyes, although, as they have interbred with Indo-Nepalese groups, some of them are tall and big-boned with open eyes, and some look strongly Semitic. As I have noted, they are the country's finest craftsmen. They are also keen astrologers, and never go off on a journey or make a major decision without first consulting the stars. They love flowers, and in Pokhara decorate their house fronts with tall, bright red Lalipata bushes— these are known in the West as the Christmas Star poinsettia.

Although both Buddhist and Hindu, the Newars have accepted the orthodox caste system: farmers, traders, and craftsmen are high on the list, butchers and sweepers way at the bottom. The mountains above them figure strongly also, of course, in their mythology. Any people who live in the shadow of such vast, mysterious, awesome giants are bound to invent stories about them and invest them with supernatural qualities. The Newars, for instance, believe that two goddesses live at the summit of Machha Puchhare, though it looks even sharper than the Matterhorn—and a rather uncomfortable place for even goddesses to dwell!

Sometimes the mountains shine like polished silver, sometimes they seem to be aflame in the glow of the setting sun, sometimes their crests are hidden behind great plumes of clouds. Color and shape are in such constant change, with such endless variety, that I often felt, as I stood gazing up at them, that these stern great giants were playing games with me.

The name Annapurna means "food-giver," and it is easy to see

why: the great rivers that gush out of the snowy mountains are an endless source of water for irrigation, even when the lowland rivers further south have all dried up. Machha Puchhare, as I have already noted, means fish-tail, and it is not so easy to see why from Pokhara, but if you walk two or three days to the west, you see that the summit is split by a crevice into two curved forms that do, indeed, resemble the tail of a fish—or the inverted head of a spear.

In the spring of 1957, a British expedition got within a hundred and fifty feet of the summit of Machha Puchhare but then had to turn back because of bad weather. A French expedition, under Herzog, made the first successful ascent of Annapurna in 1950.

After five days spent in and around Pokhara, Pemba and I left, with our ten porters, for Namun Bhanjyang. When we were only a couple of hours on the march, I noticed that oil was dripping from one of our cases. We halted, and I found the bottle completely empty; it had been loosely corked. So, at the first village we came to, we halted again, and I had the cases carefully repacked. I also bought some sneakers for the porters to wear in the snow.

Here in this village lived the wife of one of them—and so he had to take his farewell of her, which he was very reluctant to do. A very tender parting scene was enacted before our fascinated eyes.

After we left the town, I discovered we had forgotten some chickens I had bought, so I sent a porter back for them—but not the one who had just left a desolate wife. I was afraid a second parting scene might be too much for him.

Near the upper stream of Madi Khola lie terraced farms, and

the path leads through fields and villages. The heat here was intense. The porters walked very slowly and took frequent halts; whenever they saw a stand by the way, they stopped for a cup of tea and a rest.

Toward evening, I was walking alongside the bereaved porter—the others had gone on ahead of us. As we began to approach the starting point for the ascent of Namun Bhanjyang, the porter told me he was too tired to go on. I asked a villager if he had happened to see the other porters but could not understand his dialect. I decided we had better make camp there anyway.

The porter, breathing hard, put down his load, and we had just started to settle in, when I saw lights in the distance. It was a clear, starry night. Soon Pemba appeared, with three other porters, who took up the cases again, and led me to the camp that they had already prepared. Supper was ready, and as we ate, the other porters teased the lonely one who had refused to go on. There was much loud, coarse laughter in the flickering light—as though it was all the greatest joke in the world.

The next morning, after we crossed the Madi Khola, the real ascent began, and it was very steep. Once, during one of our frequent rests, an old farmer came up to me and said, in surprisingly good English, "Good morning. How are you? Are you going to Bhanjyang?" His English, in fact, was far better than Pemba's. As our conversation went on, I discovered that he was a Gurkha who had been with the British at Imphal during the Second World War. Although he had fought against us, he admired and liked the Japanese, and was delighted to hear that I was from Tokyo.

The first Gurkhas were recruited by the British as long ago as 1814. At one point, the Gurkha Brigade was made up of ten regiments of two battalions each, but by the end of the Second World War, there were forty-five Gurkha battalions fighting with the British in Africa as well as Asia, and on nearly all the fronts. In Burma, we Japanese learned how proficient they were at jungle fighting.

Actually, although the British called all the Nepalese soldiers they recruited Gurkhas, most of them belonged to other ethnic groups, such as the Thamangs, the Rais, the Gurungs, and so on.

The name comes from the little town of Gurkha, in central Nepal, where Prithwi Narayan, in 1766, began his successful campaign to subjugate the country. It was then that the Gurkhas imposed their language, Gurkhali, on the new kingdom as its national tongue. And perhaps that is why the British, later on, called all the soldiers they recruited, and indeed all Nepalese, Gurkhas.

Five thousand feet above the town of Gurkha stands the holy castle that is associated with Goraknath, one of the eighty-four Grand Magicians of tantrism, who gave his name to the Gurkhas. Goraknath, angered when the people in the region refused to worship him, hid himself away in a cave under the castle, where he contrived to get all the rain spirits into his power. As a result, no rain fell in the valley of Nepal for a full year, and men and animals alike were dying of the drought, when the king hit upon a plan to appease Goraknath by reanimating the magician's *guru*. It was a complicated scheme, but apparently it worked, for rain fell again in central Nepal, and today pilgrims climb all the many steep stone steps to worship in the cave of Goraknath.

In the valley of the Marsyandi, I met another farmer who had once been a British soldier; he had been to Hongkong and had traveled through Indonesia. I asked him if he could speak Malay. *"Terima kaseh, tuan,*" he replied, which means "Thank you, sir." I confess I had never expected to hear Malay spoken by a Nepalese in the deep Himalayas!

It was in 1947, when India became independent, that the Gurkha Brigade was broken up. Six of its regiments joined the new Indian army, while four stayed with the British. These latter were conspicuous in dealing with the Communist insurrections in Malaya, and it was there that my friend, the Nepalese farmer, learned to speak his Malay.

With a distant look of longing in his eyes, he told me that once he had loved a beautiful young Indonesian girl—now, he said, he had a quarrelsome wife and three children. No more beautiful young Indonesian girls for him! As we parted, I felt a moment of poignant nostalgia for my own youth too. . . .

We climbed on and on, and suddenly found ourselves in a strange dark forest, its trees festooned with a kind of Spanish moss. The porters told me that there were leopards in the forest, but, though we saw their pad marks, we caught no glimpse of the animals themselves.

The ascent to Namun Bhanjyang, which lies almost twenty thousand feet above sea level, is very steep. Almost at the top, however, tired as I was, I was so excited that I ran the rest of the way. The view was, indeed, spectacular—more so than I can possibly describe in words. Annapurna and Lamjung Himal towered high into the heavens across the valley, while opposite, Manaslu reared its sharp-cut profile. Unfortunately, toward the east, it was foggy: Himal Chuli and P29 Peak stood invisible beneath their gray blankets.

We camped on the grassland. That night it snowed, and the next morning a thick white carpet lay everywhere. The shivering porters said they were glad we had got to Namun Bhanjyang yesterday and not today. And how pleased they were to have the sneakers I had bought for them at Pokhara!—even though the shoes, they said, rubbed against the tops of their feet. The porters' soles were very tough, like the soles of shoes, for they customarily went barefoot, but the tops of their feet were very tender, and bruised easily with the friction of the shoes.

The water that flowed into the lake below Manaslu was so cold, one felt one's hand might drop off if one touched it. The reflection of Manaslu in the clear icy water was an incomparable sight.

I spent the day taking pictures. Everywhere I looked was so awe-inspiring, every vista so magnificent, I felt I oughtn't even take time out to breathe! The huge, pyramid-shaped rocks changed color from moment to moment as the sun shifted over them in its path. The west side of Manaslu's P29 Peak, across the valley of the Marsyandi, looked as though it had been sliced clean by some god wielding a gigantic knife.

One of my porters told me how to go around Namun Bhanjyang's peak and down into the Marsyandi valley, but though we followed his instructions, we lost our way in a thick fog and that night made camp without knowing where we were. The next morning, I was shocked to see the sun rising from the direction of the descending path. But it was too late now to go back to Pokhara, so we walked on for two days, unsure of our direction, until at last we reached the Marsyandi river. It was not the warmest walk I have ever made, and as the waters of the Marsyandi come, in large part, from the glaciers above, it is not the warmest river in the world either.

The porters had found a little stall beside the path that sold *chang*, the local rice-beer, and that night they all proceeded to get drunk. (I paid for the *chang*, by the way.) And for supper that night, instead of the customary chicken, we had a feast of mutton. It was portioned out with the most scrupulous care, and not a scrap was wasted. I even saw one porter washing the sheep's entrails in a stream (while another porter, right beside him, washed his underwear!).

In the ten days I had been with them, I had come to know my porters well. Jesse, their leader, was—as a leader apparently must be—a man of strong character. Shelbadol, who had charge of my camera on its tripod, was even-tempered and merry by disposition but extremely conscientious about the job that had been entrusted to him. The porter who carried our tents, though still very young, was the richest of the lot—for he was their best card-player: when I paid their wages, he collected from each the money he had won in the past few days. One old fellow, with a topknot on his head, habitually wore a worried expression, as though he had all the weight of the world on his shoulders. The Sherpa, Pemba, was, as I had feared, too easy-going to be an effective boss of the porters.

We continued on, around the north of Annapurna, in the direction of Muktinath and Tukuche, although I knew that we would be able to complete the trip only if we passed inspection at the checkpoint in the village of Thonje. I had been told, by friends in Kathmandu, that the Thonje checkpoint was often difficult.

We reached a little village deep in a ravine, where one could only catch occasional glimpses of the mountains. As in the Japanese mountain villages of Shinshu, the roofs of the houses were made of stone.

Here we were greeted by a big man in uniform, a Nepalese captain, accompanied by a soldier: they had heard of our arrival and had come out from the Thonje checkpoint to meet us. The soldier asked me for my passport and the card that gave me permission to travel, which I handed to him and which he handed to the captain, who studied both documents carefully.

I told him that I had come from Japan to take pictures of the mountains, and that I hoped to get back to Pokhara by way of Tukuche. He said in order to do that I would have to pass through Muktinath and the Jomosom checkpoint. Inasmuch as this was precisely what I wanted to do, I agreed with alacrity, thankful that everything had gone so well and that my apprehensions—at least so far—had been groundless.

Then we settled down to a conversation. The captain told me he had once been stationed at Namche Bazar, in the Everest region, so we talked about that for a bit, and then we got onto the subject of the delights of Kathmandu. When I remarked how delicious the beer was, he said they had some good beer right there in the village. "Is it *chang*?" I asked. "It's mountain beer," he replied, with a laugh, and led me off to a house where a shabby old woman opened the *chang*-keg. I didn't much like the way she mixed it with water in the cup and stirred it with a grubby finger, but I thought, out of politeness, I had better drink it. And when, once again out of politeness, I remarked that it was good, the captain poured me another cup, although he himself, being on duty, refused to drink. Another cup of *chang* led to another cup of *chang*, and soon I began to feel quite exhilarated. The old woman refused to accept money, so I gave her some Jintan, a Japanese breath-sweetener, and told her it was a very expensive medicine.

We set up camp on the outskirts of the village, beside the stone-roofed houses. As the porters wanted to do some shopping in the village, I paid their wages—a fairly lengthy process, since I carried only one-rupee coins with me. The porters, that evening, went to the village with their money bags filled; when they came back, their money bags were empty—and they had brought some *chang* for me, as a present.

We continued on, toward Muktinath, passing village after village. Once, at a bridge, I saw fifteen lamas repeating their prayer: *om mani padme hum*. As I was taking pictures of them, one of the lamas looked up to smile when he heard me say, *"Manne, manne."* This is a kind of small prayer-wheel used by Tibetan lamas.

And one night, after we made camp, we were visited by four villagers who had been chopping wood beside the path along which we had marched earlier. They were wearing their winter clothes, made of silk, with matching hats, on which pictures of the Dalai Lama had been sewn. They were, I learned, members of the Khamba tribe who, during the Tibetan disturbances, had taken refuge in Mustang for two years before coming to this particular village. They wanted some medicine from me—three of them had colds, and one had a sizable lump on his neck. I gave them what I could.

Next morning, three more villagers came seeking medicine.

THE HIMALAYAS 业

These people who live in the remote places of Nepal, having heard of the wonders of modern drugs, regard every traveling foreigner as a doctor of medicine and all who are ill apply to him for treatment. Alas, how many there are! It is a sad fact that the average Nepalese life span is only twenty-six years. And three quarters of the population have never consulted a doctor, although all the infectious diseases that proliferate in the tropics—typhoid, cholera, dysentery, malaria—are rife. No wonder they come to us "medicine-men" from the outside world, hoping for miracles.

I gave the three villagers what I could, but I could not be lavish, as I really did not have enough for myself and the porters should any emergency arise.

As we approached the village of Manangbhot, we saw—through a thick dust storm—the magnificent white summits of Annapurna towering on our left. Then suddenly we heard the sound of women singing. We stopped and waited, and soon a group of girls came into sight, singing as they marched down the path. They seemed quite astonished at first to see us, but after they had recovered their composure, they told us they were bringing salt from Manang to Thonje, to exchange for grain. My porters began to tease them; soon there was much shouting and laughter; the porters pretended they were going to steal the potatoes that the girls had brought for their lunch, and this produced more jokes and more laughter. At last, the girls went off, still singing. We watched them until they disappeared into the swirling dust.

After crossing the Thorungtse Pass—a long, hard walk, some fifteen thousand feet above sea level—we came onto a desert-like plateau, all dry and bare. As I was trying to capture the strange beauty of it on film, a lama came by on horseback, accompanied by a young boy. They too were of the Khamba tribe, and greeted us with the words, "*Namestey, namestey.*" The lama was carrying a box full of pictures of the Dalai Lama. He offered me wine, with the remark that it was the best thing to drink in this cold country, and I gave him in return some Jintan. Then he made a little speech, saying that his people were struggling against Communist China and that, with the help of the United States and India, they would surely win. His was a sad, noble face, and as we parted I wished him well.

We reached Muktinath at last, where we spent three days. To Muktinath, which is in Thakali territory, and which stands some twelve thousand feet above sea level, come pilgrims from all over Nepal, as well as India and Tibet, to worship in the temple of Jwala Mai. In this temple there burns a flame fed by natural gas that issues through a fissure in the rock, and as a gush of water flows from the same aperture, it appears that the water itself is miraculously burning. The sight is considered to be a sign of divine omnipotence. We were ushered into the sacred inner temple by an old woman who was both guide and guardian. There, through flickering candle-light, I saw images of Siva and of other Hindu gods. Pemba and the porters knelt reverently before them, and before the miraculously burning water. After I had taken a few pictures, I made a donation of five rupees; and so did Pemba.

Muktinath has, also, a small, pagoda-type temple of Vishnu, with a hundred and eight sacred water spouts, and two other temples, one Buddhist and one Hindu; but they were all too much alike in character for me to be able to distinguish one from the other.

Cold wintry blasts swept down from the mountains as we left Muktinath for the Kali Gandaki valley, and perhaps it was this intense cold that made the porters walk faster. When we neared the river, the wind blew so hard and there was such a thick cloud of dust, we could not keep our eyes open. It was one of the most difficult crossings I have ever made.

By the bank of the river stood a *chang* stall which, I can tell you, we were all very happy to see: after we had had a cup or two, we began to feel somewhat more human.

The Kali Gandaki (called also the Krishna Gandaki) means the "black river." It rises in a lake near the Tibetan border and flows down to the Ganges, and so is part of an important trade route. Most of the commerce along it is conducted by the shrewd and prosperous Thakals.

While we were still drinking our *chang*, we were joined by a Thakal trader who had with him ten sheep bearing rock salt strapped to their backs. It was his intention, presumably, to dispose eventually of both the salt and its bearers.

In early evening, we entered the village of Jomosom, another checkpoint. There I met several policemen, who invited me into their office but who seemed quite uninterested in looking at my passport or my permission card. They were delighted, they said, to have a visitor from Japan, and offered me *rakshi*, a strong spirit made of rice and millet. The chief of the policemen, an extremely likable man, was named Basnet; his wife, who had also joined us, was a woman of obviously strong character who held her liquor with the best of them. We consumed a rather fearful amount of *rakshi* before calling it a night.

The next morning, I met the captain of the checkpoint, who told me that drinking was, after all, the chief diversion of the people stationed here in the heart of the icy mountains. Then Basnet showed me around the village, where I met a Sherpa who had been with the Kyoto University expedition to Ganesh. He had come to Jomosom on business, and told me that in Tukuche, en route to Jomosom, he had met two Japanese and two Sherpas. One of these two Sherpas, I discovered, was Dawathondup, an old man whom I had met on my first Himalayan journey. I said I very much hoped that I too would run into them, in Tukuche or on the trail.

As we talked on, this Sherpa mentioned that friends of his in the Khamba tribe were going to try to get hold of thirty gold statues of the Buddha, which he would then sell in India. (I wondered if he was going to have to smuggle them across the border, for India has strict regulations against the importation of gold.) I remarked, quite casually, that in any case I would like to have one, and sure enough, when we met again some time later in Kathmandu, he remembered my remark and gave me one of the statues—which I still, of course, have.

In early afternoon, our drinking party started again. The minute one *rakshi* bottle was empty, another was opened. Some Nepalese soldiers joined us and soon began to sing and dance; then Basnet's wife sang a sad love-song of the Krishna Gandaki; and at last I made my contribution—a Japanese loach-scooping dance called the Dojō Sukui. And still the *rakshi* flowed on. I only hope everybody had as good a time as I did.

Unfortunately, we had to set off very early the next morning, but despite the early hour (and the late night) all our friends came down to see us off. Basnet and his wife were joining us because they had to go to Baglung for the men's salary. The others stood waving till we were out of sight. They were such happy, warm, sympathetic people, I was almost moved to tears at having to say goodbye to them.

I have read an account that a Buddhist priest, Keikai Kawaguchi, wrote in 1899 of a journey along the path that we were now taking. He complains of the loose morals of the people in the area and says that there were villages where white slavery was rife.

I don't suppose it exists any longer (if it ever did), but I do know that in Nepal, as in the other countries of the world, there are places where the women are noted for their beauty. I have been, for example, to the village of Tarkeghyang, in the district of Helmu, where the Ranas lived when they were in power. They brought to their palace at one time some three thousand of the most beautiful girls they could find anywhere—and so the women of Tarkeghyang have, not at all unnaturally, acquired a reputation for great beauty.

As we arrived at the very pretty village of Thinigaon, I cried, "Schön! Schön!" I then explained to Basnet how we Japanese sometimes use that German word to refer to a pretty girl. He turned and looking at his wife echoed, "Schön! Schön!"

At Thinigaon, I met the two Japanese I had been told about, and I was also able to shake hands again with old Dawathondup. When I told him that he was looking well, he smiled and said, "*Sahab salam.*" After an all-too-brief chat with my fellow-Japanese travelers, who had to be on their way, I spent the night in the house of a friend of Basnet's. The *rakshi* bottle made its usual instant appearance.

Unhappily, the son of the house had cut his foot with an ax, while chopping wood, and the wound had got infected. The boy had been in bed for several days with a fever. The family asked my advice, but alas! I was neither physician nor surgeon, and could only give him some of the drugs that I had brought with me. I feared that if the infection got any worse, part of his leg might have to be amputated. But who would do it?

We continued on, early the next morning, in bitter cold. When we reached the river, one of the porters found an ammonite. These black fossil shells are very common here and seem to be proof that the High Himalayas, in the dim pre-historic past, lay at the bottom of the sea. The local people attribute magical properties to these petrifactions, which they call "*saligrams*," and believe that gold can be extracted from them. The "gold" may be the glitter of the calcium in the shells. In any case, we collected all we could before we moved on.

We caught up with some beggars walking along the valley of the river. These people, apparently, beg their way up to the very heart of the mountain in the summer and then back to Pokhara in wintertime. One of them was smoking a cigarette that he had got from a porter.

We camped next near the village of Lete, where the houses are all painted white. Hanging from the windows were dried yellow

pumpkins which, I was interested to learn, are called *"ka bocha"* here, as they are in Japan.

Pemba went several times to the village in search of *chang*. When he was successful, he would come back saying, *"Sahab, chang uta."* Now, *uta* is the word for "awake," while *niro* means "asleep." If there was no *chang* to be had, Pemba would say, *"Chang niro."*

One night, the children of the local school gave a party for us in their classroom. They did a traveler's song for me, which Basnet elucidated, and then Basnet's wife danced the Dalmyer amid much shouting.

Tukuche lies in a flat valley between Annapurna and Dhaulagiri, and is the main resting-place between the two mountains. It is not a town of great interest, save for the strangeness of the incredibly steep mountains rising on both sides of it, and for the nearby gorge of Kali Gandaki, probably the deepest in the world. Tukuche is just outside the monsoon country and still boasts a few pines and larches, but nothing grows in the valley north of it but stunted bushes and desert grass.

I took some more pictures of Churen Himal from Gurja Himal, to the west of Dhaulagiri, and then we came along the south of Annapurna to Pokhara. From Pokhara I returned to Kathmandu—which, after my two months in the high white silent mountains, glittered like a great worldly metropolis.

🌺   🌺   🌺

As everyone knows, Mount Everest is the highest peak in the High Himalayas—and the highest in the world. The struggle to "conquer" it lasted one full century, from its discovery, so-called, in 1852 by the Survey of India to the Hunt Expedition in 1953, when Sir Edmund Hillary, a New Zealander, and Tenzing Norkey, a Sherpa, made the first successful ascent. This was the eighth attempt on Everest (in addition to three reconnaissance parties), and the story of these various expeditions forms one of the most exciting chapters in the history of man's brave, indomitable desire to learn all he can about the world in which he lives.

The highest mountain in the world was named Everest in 1856 in honor of Sir George Everest, the British surveyor and geographer who was employed on surveys of India and whose geodetical work on Everest is unparalleled in its field. The local name for the entire Everest group, among both Tibetans on the north and Sherpas to the south, is Chomolongma: Mother-Goddess of the World.

The summit is 29,028 feet above sea level.

I visited the Everest area first in 1958, and now, after a short rest in Kathmandu, I began my second trip just after New Year's Day.

I had recruited ten porters for the trip, but on the morning of departure, twenty-five appeared, including three Sherpa women. As they were on their way to their home village in the Everest region, they were willing to work for only six rupees a day. Two of the women, Pema and Namdo, both young girls, were accompanied by fathers and brothers.

I took with me also two Sherpa guides: Angstering, an older man whom I felt I could trust to act as leader, and a young fellow named Temde.

Most of the porters were Mongolian natives of the Solu Khumbu district who had emigrated long ago from Tibet, and as the Japanese are also members of the Mongolian group of peoples, we all looked very much alike—and I think perhaps some of our ideas were alike too, though I came from Tokyo and they from the high mountains of Tibet.

One of their customs, however, was strange to me. On the morning after we made our first camp in the very high altitudes, the Sherpa women rose from their sleep stark naked—which woke me, I think, more quickly than any steaming cup of tea could have done. I discovered that because of the cold they slept together in the nude, and they thought nothing, apparently, of waking in the nude either. I hoped nothing untoward would happen to them.

The Everest trek is by no means an easy one: it took us eighteen days to reach Namche Bazar, our major stop. We passed through many small villages en route and forded a number of swift-flowing streams. A couple of the bridges are of iron, but most are wood, and these sometimes, in the heavy monsoons, are carried away; then the district is isolated for months from the rest of the world. Ringmo Khola has a very swift current which can only with the very greatest difficulty be waded through.

The important village markets are usually on Saturday, and for the most part only local products are sold: rice, pulse, eggs, chickens, *ghee* (clarified butter), oil, spices, onions, and potatoes. There are very few fresh vegetables to be had. One is also likely to find cheap cigarettes, kerosene, and rough mountain clothes—and that's about it.

We crossed the Midlands first, with their rice paddies and maize fields, and at Jiri had a splendid view of Mount Gauri Shankar (23,440 feet). Then, after the tropical Likhi Khola valley, we climbed to Dudh Kunda, one of the most spectacular stops on the trip—for it is almost twelve thousand feet high and offers an amazing vista of the central Himalayan snow peaks at close range.

At one of our resting places, we met six Tibetans, all with strong, rugged mountain faces, four men and two women accompanied by a rather unattractive looking dog. One woman carried a bamboo basket, in which lay a child wrapped in rags; the other was old, incredibly shabby, with the look of a witch. Her blouse was torn, and her breasts exposed. Temde told me that these were members of the lowest Tibetan caste: butchers who would slaughter a cow for four rupees and a sheep for two. No one of a higher caste (which included most of the people in their world) would sit down to eat with them. While we were preparing our own food, the old woman took off her torn blouse and went about begging from the people in our party. Two days later, we happened to meet this same group at a camping site. As luck would have it, we were short of food at the time, so my porters asked the old woman to forage some for them. They were willing, after all, to eat the food she provided—though they would not eat with her.

Angstering kept telling me that this region was infested with thieves, and since crime is so rare in Nepal, I assumed that the thieves would be people from other parts of the world, like our Tibetan butchering friends. Angstering insisted that we keep our lights on all night, as he said otherwise the thieves would sneak into our tents while we were asleep and steal everything we had.

The whole of my little party was addicted to *chang*, and since the Everest route is a well-traveled one, the *chang* stalls are numerous. And so were our stops. It seems that the Nepalese simply cannot live in this cold, rarefied part of the world without their *chang*. Even the young girls were heavy drinkers. And they all, I am afraid, had the habit of stopping to drink without permission and then expecting me to pay for what they had had!

THE HIMALAYAS ❧

Once, a girl at one of the stalls asked Temde, the young Sherpa, to step inside. When he came out again, after a while, he said, "This *chang* no good," and as he was quite red in the face, I assume he had sampled enough of it to decide whether it was palatable or not.

While we walked, of course we talked. I heard many a tale of Sherpa life as we went along. Temde, for instance, told me that if a Sherpa couple have no children after several years of marriage, the woman has the right no longer to call herself the man's wife. It appears that, despite the fact that the two were formally married, the time between the wedding-day and the day the first child is born is actually considered to be a trial period. If the marriage is barren, presumably they stop trying and change partners.

The woman who bears the most children is considered to be the best wife—but in actual fact, Sherpa families are quite small. In the Khumbu valley, for instance, there were twenty-two hundred people living in six hundred houses.

Much of our talk, as always in Sherpa country, was about the Yeti—the "abominable snowman." He is a constant theme in Sherpa conversation, particularly at night, as the lights flicker and the winds howl, and I suppose in Sherpa thoughts as well—though no one I have ever spoken to has admitted actually seeing him. It is always grandfather's brother who glimpsed him once, some years back, or perhaps mother's uncle—never the man you are talking to.

Yet it seems quite clear that he actually does exist. His footprints were first found and photographed in 1951, and they are unquestionably those of a living biped, though what he is, monkey or ape, or bear perhaps, no one knows. The skins that were exhibited as his were later shown to be fraudulent.

Some people believe that when the Yeti is at last found, if he ever is, he will prove to be the long-sought and so-called "missing link." The theory is that when the Himalayas rose to their present height, at the end of the Tertiary period, their forests began to die and the apes who lived in them were forced to come down out of the trees and learn to live on the ground. That was how they acquired the ability to walk erect on their hind legs—an ability that eventually changed the shape of their skull and enlarged their brain capacity. It is, of course, man's greater brain that gives him what he likes to think of as his preeminence in the world.

But whatever the Yeti is, missing link or great bear, he figures prominently in Sherpa talk. Lhakpatenzing told me that when he was with an American expedition, he saw footprints that the Yeti had left but a few hours before. Pasang Phuttar believes that any man who sees the Yeti will become obsessed by evil spirits. Angstering said there were two kinds of Yeti and imitated the cries of each: these noises so terrified the other Sherpas that the women refused to go out to the toilets.

Another old man, from the village of Thame, told me that while he was leading a herd of yak to another village, one of them disappeared. He was convinced that the Yeti had carried it off. But it is not only yak that the Yeti carries off: once he came and feasted on all the people in a mountain hut (there were no survivors), and he has often kidnaped little girls.

His exploits grow more daring, and more frightening, as the winds grow louder in the icy Himalayan nights.

At Jugal, I always carried a camera with a telephoto lens ready, in case anyone sighted the Yeti in the far distance—but like every other Himalayan photographer, I came back without him.

THE HIMALAYAS 🌸

If the Nepalese have a snowman, I decided, they ought to have a snow-woman too, so I told the Sherpas a story about a snow fairy who lives in the north of Japan. The Sherpas said they too had a snow-woman: she is called Tsurin in Nepalese and Demo in Sherpa and she is not at all abominable—at least to look at, for like all snow fairies she is of an enchanting beauty. At night she appears in the mountains to young men and beckons them to follow her; those who do, never return. I said I hoped to meet her some night. Even if I didn't follow her, I could at least take her picture— for I had plenty of flash bulbs!

We began now to approach Angstering's native country, and his face brightened as he greeted old friends and told me their stories. He was particularly impressed with a very wise old man of great renown among the Sherpas whose name was Pasang Phuttar.

In the Solu Khumbu district, we met another eminent Sherpa named Wilkieng, who was now a kind of counselor to his fellow tribesmen. He was a fat man whose family had once been wealthy merchants, and he himself had often crossed the Himalayas, bringing corn, rice, and sugar to exchange for the expensive and much desired Tibetan tea. Then, he told me, he discovered he could buy more tea in Tibet if he had with him a thick wad of money— so, in order to make his wallet thicker, he decided to print the money himself. Shortly afterwards, these bright new notes were seen everywhere, and shortly after that, Wilkieng was arrested on suspicion of counterfeiting. But his fellow Sherpas went to the magistrates to plead on his behalf, and they succeeded in freeing him and bringing him back. I could never quite decide whether to believe Wilkieng's story or not.

At long last, after eighteen days of hard marching, we reached Namche Bazar, the main Sherpa village in this part of Everest and the largest market in the region, where mountaineers can replenish their stocks. I even found some powdered milk that a Sherpa told me had been given him by one of the three parties that had already visited Namche Bazar that spring.

The village is not quite ten thousand feet above sea level and has about a hundred houses. It is in constant contact, apparently, with Tibet—although the frontier was officially closed.

We went on, of course, to Thyangboche, some two hours (six miles) away from Namche Bazar and some two thousand feet higher. It lies at the top of a hill overlooking the Dudh Kosi and Imja Khola valley. From it, the views of Everest are awesome and stupendous, with the highest peak towering above the snowy ridges that join Lhotse and Nhuptse and other lesser peaks.

During the winter, the whole area is frozen solid and covered with thick snow. The people bury their potatoes in the fields to keep them from freezing and dig up what they need each day. *Tsampa* is also a common food here. All the men and women in the region, and even the children, work when they can as guides and porters for mountain-climbing parties, sometimes going as far as Kathmandu and sometimes all the way to the Indian frontier.

When the men are off, the women not only do the housework and the weaving but labor in the fields as well. It was from this kind of family that our Sherpa girls came. They seemed to have weathered the trip well, and to have suffered no (at least apparent) ill effects from sleeping in the nude! (continued on page 58)

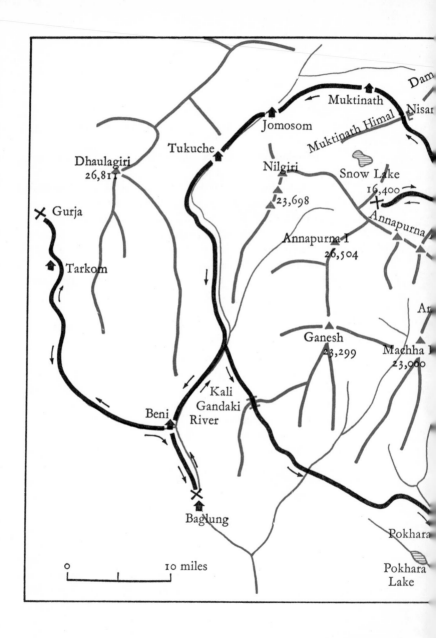

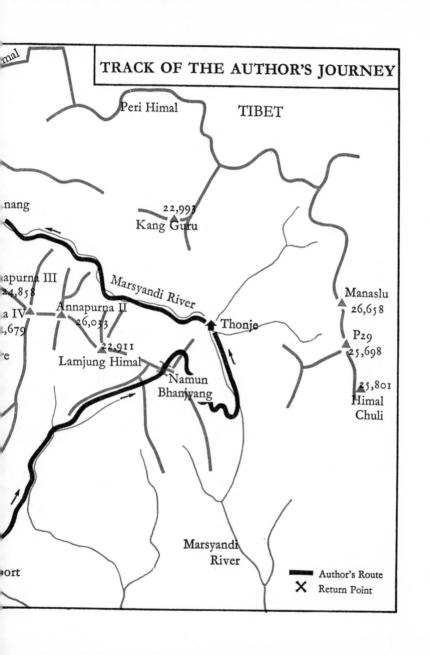

TRACK OF THE AUTHOR'S JOURNEY

Peri Himal

TIBET

nang

22,993
Kang Guru

apurna III
24,858

Marsyandi River

Manaslu
26,658

Annapurna II
26,033

a IV
,679

Thonje

P29
25,698

e

22,911
Lamjung Himal

25,801
Himal
Chuli

Namun
Bhanjyang

Marsyandi
River

ort

▬▬▬ Author's Route
✗ Return Point

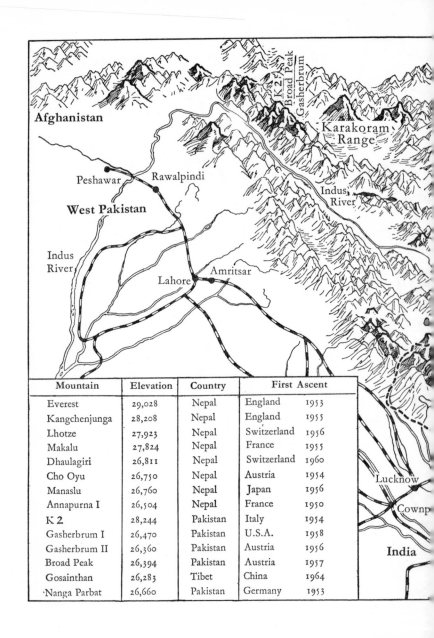

Mountain	Elevation	Country	First Ascent	
Everest	29,028	Nepal	England	1953
Kangchenjunga	28,208	Nepal	England	1955
Lhotze	27,923	Nepal	Switzerland	1956
Makalu	27,824	Nepal	France	1955
Dhaulagiri	26,811	Nepal	Switzerland	1960
Cho Oyu	26,750	Nepal	Austria	1954
Manaslu	26,760	Nepal	Japan	1956
Annapurna I	26,504	Nepal	France	1950
K 2	28,244	Pakistan	Italy	1954
Gasherbrum I	26,470	Pakistan	U.S.A.	1958
Gasherbrum II	26,360	Pakistan	Austria	1956
Broad Peak	26,394	Pakistan	Austria	1957
Gosainthan	26,283	Tibet	China	1964
·Nanga Parbat	26,660	Pakistan	Germany	1953

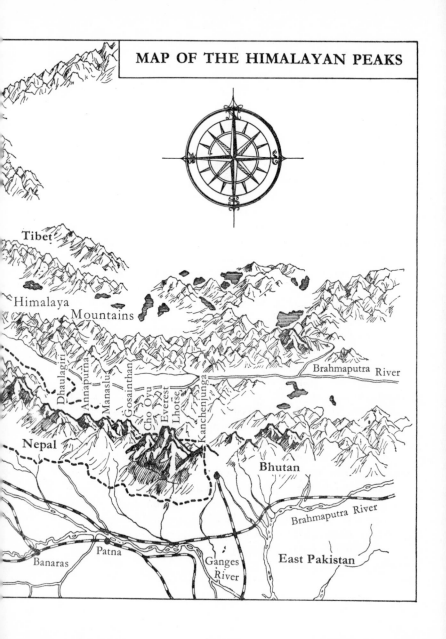

MAP OF THE HIMALAYAN PEAKS

Tibet

Himalaya
Mountains

Brahmaputra River

Dhaulagiri
Annapurna
Manaslu
Gosainthan
Cho Oyu
Everest
Lhotse
Kanchenjunga

Nepal

Bhutan

Brahmaputra River

Patna

Banaras

Ganges
River

East Pakistan

THE HIMALAYAS

The Monastery of Thangboche stands some little distance from the village itself, its golden spire glittering in the bright mountain sun. One of the young lamas fell madly in love with Pema, but her response seemed to me to be rather cool. This did not, however, deter him from coming often to see her (we stayed in the region for a month and a half), and when I left, he asked me to take a picture of them together. Some time later, I put the photograph in the mails—and thought of the strangeness of a love affair between a young Buddhist monk and a Sherpa girl-porter high in the High Himalayas. At the time, however, it seemed the most natural thing in the world.

When the unhappy time came for me to leave, in order to get back to Kathmandu before the monsoon season began, all the people I had known came to see me off, though for many of them it meant a day's walk. Some brought me bottles of *chang*, and one kind soul gave me a white lace necklace as an amulet to ward off evil spirits. How sad I felt when the day of parting finally came! It seemed to me I had never known such simple, honest, kindly people—and I remember them still with the deepest affection.

I returned to Kathmandu by way of Biratnagar, an industrial city of over thirty thousand, where the world began to close in on me again and the pure white mountains to fade away into treasured memories. Back in the capital, though I had been away so short a time, there already seemed to be more cars on the streets than when I had left. Kathmandu was beginning to be a place for tourists to visit—and probably, like everywhere else in the world, would never be the same again.

4. *Manga Deocali Pass* affords a splendid view of the Eastern Himalayas. The high peak is Gaurishanker, which was once thought to be Everest, though the latter is actually almost six thousand feet higher. The peak to the right is Menlungtse.

5. *My Sherpa porters*, on the trek to Everest, included fifteen who were on their way home to their villages in the Everest region. When I saw them all lined up, I felt like the leader of a major expedition!

6. *The Himalayan spring* reminded ▶ me of springtime in my own Japanese countryside. Here, in the Dudh Kosi River valley, against a background of the high mountains, are rape flowers in blossom.

8. *Taksindhu Pass*, with a couple of the many ancient chortens that are found in profusion here. It is only a few days' walk to Namche Bazar, Everest's chief market.

9. *The Kwangde Peak*, as seen from Namche Bazar. On the chorten on the left, is a painted face that stares impartially at passing travelers and giant mountains.

◀7. *The village of Junbesi*, in Sherpa country, with white-walled houses and white lamaist shrines (called chortens) in a ravine. The mountain towering in the background is Numbur, first conquered by a Japanese expedition.

10. *In the village of Khunde,* cows head slowly off toward the fields, looking for pasture. This picture was taken on a bitterly cold winter morning, with a sharp north wind blowing. Sometimes the whole village is covered with snow.

11. *Mount Ama Dablam* rearing▶ its giant crest in the far distance. In the foreground, the Sherpa villages of Khunde and Khumjung, as seen from a slope of Mount Khumbui Yul Lha.

12. *Thamserku Pass* (near Namche Bazar, in the Everest region) at sunset. I stood here for a long time, excitedly watching, and photographing, the ever-changing sunset views.

13. *Two snow-capped peaks*—Kang-
tega (over nineteen thousand feet)
and Thamserku (over twenty-one
thousand feet)—changing their
shape and color every second as
the sun passes over them.

14. *Three Everest summits*—Nuptse (23,058 feet), Lhotse (27,890 feet), and Everest itself (29,028 feet)— rise behind the Imja Khola valley. In the foreground yaks are feeding on the plateau where the Thangboche Monastery stands.

15. *The Monastery of Thangboche*, with Ama Dablam in the background, its crest like a giant face. The Hunt Expedition used the slope to the right in its successful assault on Everest; two lives were lost in the Ama Dablam glacier.

16. *Thangboche Monastery*, another view (*see overleaf*), with neighboring buildings clustered at its feet. After the gates of Nepal were thrown open in 1950, British and Swiss expeditions used Thangboche as a starting-point for their Himalayan ascents. In the background, above a cloud in the valley, rises Kwangde Peak.

17—18. *Wall-paintings* in a *gonpa* (a Tibetan Buddhist monastery). To the left, is the artist's vision of Heaven; below, his vision of Hell.

74

19—21. *The world of lamaism:* another group of paintings from a *gonpa*. Lamaism is an expression of Mahayana Buddhism, called the Great Vehicle and found largely in Tibet, Nepal, China, and Japan; after the Dalai Lama was forced into exile by the Tibetan government, a number of lamas followed him to India and took refuge also in Nepal. Here can be seen a mystical expression of the Mahayana belief in universal salvation.

22. *New Year's Day* at the Monastery of Thangboche: above, a procession, in mask and costume, to celebrate the first day of the New Year, an important festival.

23. *A huge bonfire* is lit, and then paper snakes and dolls made of mud are thrown into the fire in order to drive away demons and spirits of evil.

24—25. *A lama's funeral*: here a funeral service is being conducted, in the midst of the high mountains, for an elderly lama, who had died a few days before. The word "lama" means not only a Buddhist monk or priest but any kind of superior person—all of whom may, when their deeds are tallied, hope that the next incarnation will be at least as good as the last one.

26—31. *Bakbas.* A *bakba* is a Tibetan clay mask, colored red, yellow, or blue for the most part, with a snake-design painted in. They are worn by dancers at the large outdoor festivals and are intended to represent demons and evil spirits. The Monastery of Thangboche

has a large collection of these masks, with both human and non-human faces, which it displays in a darkened room on the second floor of the building. As they are only painted clay, these masks lack the subtlety and depth of feeling of the Nō masks of my own country.

32. *Ama Dablam Peak*, in early morning, has a breathtaking grandeur and a purity that help to explain the intense religious feeling of the people who live here amongst the high mountains. Ama Dablam looks as though the hands of God Himself had carved it.

34. *The village of Khumjung* has, for ▶
Himalayan pilgrims, a kind of
Utopian reputation, and though it
does indeed look peaceful, nest-
ling on the slopes below Ama
Dablam, its high altitude may not
seem ideal to everybody.

33. *Chortens*, or lamaist shrines,
everywhere dot the narrow mountain paths. Mount Ama Dablam
rises cloud-wreathed in the background.

35. *Yaks grazing* below Mount Taboche. The chief domestic animals of the high mountain people, yaks supply milk and cheese, meat, hides and wool. The wool of the yak is short and smooth along the back, and long and wavy on the breast.

36. *Taboche Peak* rising behind▶ the village of Dingboche near the Imja Khola. Although, at twenty-one thousand feet, it is not sharply distinguished from other Everest peaks, it had the unique quality of seeming to peer down its own valley.

37. *Imja Glacier*, like other Himalayan glaciers, is less massive than might be expected, because of low precipitation and lack of névé, but it makes a magnificent contrast to the snowy peaks of Nuptse and Lhotse in the background against the dazzling blue Himalayan sky.

87

38. *The peak of Lhotse*, rising, in the center, to a height of 27,890 feet. On its left is Nuptse Peak (23,058 feet); and on the right, Lhotse Shar, which an expedition from Tokyo's Waseda University conquered, with considerable hardship, in 1965.

39. *The great giants* of the Himalayas, with their bald, black peaks, lack the tender grace of our green and wooded Japanese mountains —but they have their own icy splendor, with furiously howling winds and great drifts of snow that obliterate the way.

40. *The summit of Mount Everest* (29,028 feet) raises its crest haughtily above Mount Nuptse (only 23,058 feet), which it covers with its cold white armor.

90

42. *Khumbu Glacier*, *(see overleaf)* beyond Pangboche,▶ lies in the upper part of Khumbu Valley, the gateway to an ascent of Everest; it is mostly covered with black moraine. The Everest expedition was based mid-center in the photograph, near the pyramid-shaped blocks of snow.

41. *Mount Makalu* (*above*), the world's fifth highest mountain, lifts its pink summit behind Imja Glacier. The first successful ascent was made by a French expedition.

43. *Pumori (23,412 feet)* was first conquered by the German Himalayan Expedition in 1962. It has been called the world's most beautiful mountain.

44. *Ngojamba Glacier (below)* formed this lake through constant erosion. In winter, it freezes solid, while in summer it becomes swollen with melted ice and snow.

45. *Cho Oyu* rears its summit
(26,750 feet) behind the grassland,
watered by a glacial stream. In
summer the grassland is covered
by blossoming flowers.

46. *Beyond the black glacier* rises the vast summit of Gyadiung Kang, which was first conquered by an expedition from Nagano, when a Japanese alpinist fell to his death on April 10, 1964.

47. *An early morning view* of the mountains near Thame Khola, just after a snowfall—there is no end to the diversity of the great mountains in both form and color.

97

48. *Swayambhu Nath Sanctuary*, near Kathmandu, where images of the Buddha, Jesus, and Mahatma Gandhi stand beside those of the Hindu gods.

49. *Patan is sacred* to Hindus and Buddhists alike, whose temples are sometimes hard to distinguish from one an other; most are built in the pagoda style, which is said to be a Nepalese contribution to architecture.

50. *A Hindu god*, one of the many images to be found all over the capital city of Kathmandu, to whom the Nepalese come bearing gifts of rice, vermilion, and flowers. Hinduism sees everything in life as aspects of one eternal being, and all of Nature is sacred and inviolable.

51. *A demon-god* of the Hindus, holding a human head in one of his eight hands and wearing other human heads as attributes. It is as impossible to enumerate the Hindu gods as it is to define the religion; the chief sects center around Siva and Vishnu—who, finally, become manifestations of the ineffable Brahman.

52. *Kathmandu*, the capital of Nepal, an old city that is rapidly becoming modern. The profusion of shrines and temples reminded me of Kyoto, the ancient capital of Japan. Once the monsoon season is over, the view of the distant mountains is breathtaking in its grandeur.

53. *A morning market* in Kathmandu, where people come to buy and sell all sorts of food, perishables and staples, as well as wood and oil and the other necessities of life. Now and then a cow comes to join them, eating what she pleases as she passes by a vegetable stall, for she is as sacred here as she is to India.

54—55. *Street vendors* are seen everywhere in Kathmandu. Here, above, are men carrying unglazed pots through the streets of the capital. Below, a woman is choosing a bracelet for her daughter from a tempting array displayed by a street vendor. Nepalese women like to decorate their wrists and ears and even their noses.

56. *A porter drinking* some water offered him by a village woman. Because of the great range of altitude in Nepal, from the Terai in the south through the central plateau to the great mountains of the north, the range in climate is also very great, and portering is sometimes hot and thirsty work.

57—58. *Tibetans*, and Nepalese of more purely Tibetan stock, live far to the north, in the high mountains and the valleys of the Inner Himalayas. In the photograph above, of Tibetan men, the elderly man with all the amulets is the boss of the gang; below are young Tibetan girls, who are busy all day long, working in the fields and looking after the cattle.

59. *The view from Daman Pass* (*above*), outside of Kathmandu, with, in the far distance, Ganesh Himal in the rays of the setting sun. Ganesh Himal (23,299 feet) was conquered by a Swiss expedition in 1955.

60. *Below, Manaslu*, to the right, and Himal Chuli, on the left, were both conquered by Japanese expeditions, after a long struggle. The first successful assault on Manaslu (26,658 feet) in 1956 was the fifth Japanese attempt.

61. *Glare of the sun*, reflected from the snow, is one of the many hazards of high mountain climbing. Here a porter, eschewing sunglasses, protects his eyes with the fringe from his headband.

62. *Another hazard* of mountain climbing is the ever-present possibility of falling into a glacial crevasse. We picked our way carefully across this moving ice field.

63. *Jugal Himal C3*—the third camp of Jugal Himal at some sixteen thousand feet, with my red tent against the snow. The peak itself is 23,240 feet.

64. *Phurbichyachu* (over twenty thousand feet) shines like burnished metal in the sun. Natives say the name means "great bat of the East." The big split in the foreground is a crevasse.

65. *Machha Puchhare,* in the morning sun, looks a little like the
Matterhorn in the Alps—though
it is over eight thousand feet higher. The name means "fish-tail."

67. *The lake at Pokhara* (*see next*▶ *page*), with the Annapurna range in the background, as well as reflected in the lake itself: Annapurna I, Machha Puchhare, and Annapurna III.

66. *The grassland airport* outside Pokhara affords a splendid view of Machha Puchhare, with its incredibly sharp peak etched cleanly against the clear blue mountain sky.

68. *The Himalayas* have been called the "Furrow of the World," and the name might also be applied to the terraced farms that drape their slopes. Here, rice can be seen growing below with grain in the higher areas.

69. *Nepalese women* are cheerful and hard-working. The two girls on the right are carrying firewood to the market. In the background is a pole for electric wires—a rare object in this part of the world.

70. *Village girls*, all dressed up, on their way to a festival. The girl at the left wears on her forehead red grains of rice: they symbolize happiness.

119

71. *A mountain village*, with mud roofs. In the rainier south of Nepal, houses have thatched roofs like those of Japanese farmhouses.

72. *Grinding rape-seeds*, on the outskirts of Pokhara, to make oil. Girls place rape-seeds in the stone mortar: grinding them requires both dexterity and strength.

74. *Magnolias* (*above*), seem larger than elsewhere too, and the air is strong with their fresh, lovely scent.

73. *Poinsettias* (*above*), are a favorite flower in Pokhara, where they grow in great, tree-sized bushes and are used to decorate house-fronts.

75–76. *Primroses* are seen everywhere and there are over three hundred varieties. Pictured below, left and right, are two kinds.

77. *Alpine roses* (above) grow in great profusion, and in many varieties, here in the Himalayas.

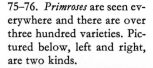

78. *Camping* near Namun Bhanjyang, the porters built a blazing fire to warm themselves against a sudden morning frost, although they had slept in the open the night before.

79. *Porters* in the High Himalayas carry about sixty pounds each, often walking barefoot across the bitterly cold ground and the snow.

80. *Kneading dough* for their ▶ lunch, porters squat in a rocky field, oblivious of the incredible autumn-tinged backdrop behind them.

81. *Lamjung Himal* (*see previous page*) changes color and shape from moment to moment as its crest emerges into the morning sunlight, over twenty-two thousand feet above sea level.

82. *Lamjung Himal:* its snow-capped summit is reflected in the water; the hill in the foreground is green in summer and covered with herds of grazing yak and sheep.

83. *Machha Puchhare:* a two-day▶ walk to the west shows how the mountain got its name, for in Nepalese *machha* means "fish" and *puchhare* means "tail"; yellow rape-blossoms bloom on the terraces in the foreground.

84.   *Heading north* from Namun Bhanjyang, one encounters this view of Manaslu and P29.

85. *Pine trees* with red ivy in the foreground; snow-capped mountains in the distance.

86. *Manaslu*, as seen from the east—a "Japanese" mountain, for it was the fifth Japanese expedition that succeeded in first attaining the summit (26,658 feet).

87. *A Himalayan farm*, near the source of the Marsyandi River, with cattle grazing in the field.

88. *The valley of the Marsyandi (see overleaf)*—▶
another view. The glacier on the right is in
the Annapurna range; the path on the left
leads to Muktinath. The village of Manangbhot, where mountaineers exploring the
Annapurna range always stop, is not far.

90. *Ngawal*: the houses in this ▶
village are built of rocks and walled
with mud; roofs are made of wood
and dried grass.

89. *The village of Braga*, which is
also near Manangbhot: cattle
graze in the fields; on the lower
slopes are the houses of the village; and above them, the temples.

91. *Nepalese boys* were not at all camera-shy, although their mothers fled, hiding their faces.

92. *Nepalese woman*—she grows all her own food and weaves her own wool.

93. *Women collect the firewood* and carry it home on their backs; the men are away, working.

94. *A caravan* on its way from Tibet, crossing the High Himalayas, with donkey-loads of rock salt to exchange for rice, wheat, and other commodities.

95. *A chorten* in the High Himalayas: natives think of these ubiquitous shrines as guardians of their villages.

96. *Prayer-stones*: "*om mani padme hum,*" say the carvings on these stones, constantly repeated; the more stones there are, the more people have been here to pray.

98. *The pass of Nisango La*, be-▶
tween Muktinath and the
Marsyandi River—although called
a "pass," this wall of dried red
earth is over fifteen thousand feet
above sea level.

97. *By the banks of the Marsyandi River*: wind, rain, and snow have carved these rocks into fanciful shapes. Eventually they will be carried away by the river.

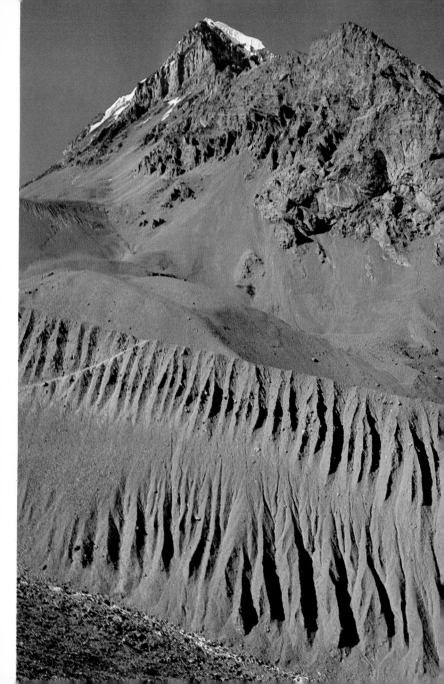

99. *Annapurna* in bright sunlight, as seen from the pass of
Nisango La—the snow at the
summit is being swirled by a storm.

100. *Annapurna* (26,504 feet) was first successfully assaulted by the French Herzog Expedition in 1950. Two of the climbers were seriously frost-bitten, and as one looks at Annapurna's intricate walls of ice, it is all too easy to see how.

101. *After Nisango La,* the world undergoes a change—from here, the way to the highlands of Tibet, the valley is dry and arid. On the right, a Tibetan-type village. In the background, the peaks of Dhaulagiri and Tukuche—one over twenty-six thousand feet, the other over twenty thousand.

102. *The village of Muktinath,* which is sacred to Hindus, with prayer-flags fluttering in the wind. As the land here is virtually tree-less, villagers must make a three-day trek down the mountain to gather firewood.

103. *A lamaist temple* in Muktinath, with a row of
cylindrical prayer-wheels, called *manne,* in the foreground.
Although Hindus come to Muktinath from all over
Nepal, as well as India and Tibet, to worship at the
shrine of Jwala Mai, there are also a number of Buddhist temples in the village.

146

104. *Another lamaist temple*, lit here by the glow of the departing sun. Many of these temples are in a state of total disrepair, with only a dusty image of the Buddha lit by a flickering candle in the ghostly silence. An old woman generally acts as guardian and guide.

147

105. *Ganesh Himal* by the light of the morning sun, its principal peak to the left. In the autumn of 1964, an expedition from Kyoto University assaulted the twenty-three-thousand-foot-high pinnacle.

106. *Churen Himal*, west of
Dhaulagiri, rears its sharp-cut
crest, as deep shadows play over
the nearer range. Churen Himal,
too, has been explored by a Japanese group.

107. *The view from Tarkom*, which
lies in a peaceful valley at the foot
of the mountains. Here there are
banana trees, and rich pasture land.

108. *A mountain market* of sheep and goats, brought from the scattered villages of the region; bargaining continues as the owners walk along the mountain paths with their herds.

109. *The Himalayan sun* has already begun to cast its morning rays over the slopes of Dhaulagiri, though the moon still hangs brightly in the sky and the glacier still lies in the shadow of night.

THIS BEAUTIFUL WORLD